Read & Res~~~~

M000251615

Ages
7~11

SECTION
1

War Horse

SECTION
2

Guided reading

SECTION
3

Shared reading

SECTION
4

Plot, character and setting

SECTION
5

Talk about it

SECTION
6

Get writing

SECTION
7

Assessment

PAGE
1

Read & Respond

Ages
7–11

Author: Jillian Powell

Commissioning Editor: Rachel Mackinnon

Development Editor: Marion Archer

Assistant Editor: Tracy Kewley

Series Designer: Anna Oliwa

Designer: Dan Prescott

Illustrations: Stephen Lillie

Text © 2011, Jillian Powell © 2011 Scholastic Ltd

Designed using Adobe InDesign

Published by Scholastic Ltd,
Book End, Range Road, Witney,
Oxfordshire OX29 0YD
www.scholastic.co.uk

Printed by Bell & Bain
456789   34567890

British Library Cataloguing-in-Publication Data
A catalogue record for this book is available from the British Library.

ISBN 978-1407-12718-7

Acknowledgements

The publishers gratefully acknowledge permission to reproduce the following copyright material:
Egmont UK Ltd. for the use of extracts and cover from *War Horse* by Michael Morpurgo. Text © 1982, Michael Morpurgo (1982, Kay & Ward Ltd). Cover © 2006, National Theatre's stage adaptation poster.
Every effort has been made to trace copyright holders for the works reproduced in this book, and the publishers apologise for any inadvertent omissions.

War Horse

About the book

War Horse is set during the First World War (1914–18). It tells the story of a farm horse sold to the British cavalry and taken to France. Before going to war the horse lives happily on an English farm with a boy called Albert, who cares for him and names him Joey. The boy's father needs money and sells the horse without telling his son. In the war, Joey's first rider is killed and, after several battles, the horse is captured. The horse is then employed by the Germans to pull ambulance carts, over-wintering on a French farm where he is cared for by a young girl before being commandeered to carry heavy German guns. While Joey labours in the war, his first owner and friend, Albert, joins the army and searches for his beloved horse. They are reunited before the end of the war and eventually travel back together to their English farm.

The horse's adventures are told in the first person, providing a poignant view of the horrors of war from an animal's point of view. Morpurgo has said that the novel was inspired by a chance encounter with a First World War veteran in his local pub in Iddesleigh, Devon. Captain Budgett, then in his eighties, had served with the Devon Yeomanry and recalled how, amidst the horrors of trench warfare, his only confidant was his horse. Morpurgo was also moved by a painting of British cavalry horses charging towards German lines in 1917, some painfully entangled in the wire. He has said that 'finding the right voice' for a story is an important part of its conception. In *War Horse*, by choosing a horse used by both armies to narrate the tale, he is able to tell the story of the Great War from neither one side nor the other – a truly non-partisan view of the futility of war.

About the author

Michael Morpurgo was a 'war baby', born in 1943 during the Second World War (1939–45). He studied English and French at London University, before becoming a primary school teacher in Kent. It was there that he realised he wanted to write, when he discovered he found 'magic' in inventing stories for the children. His first book was published in 1975 and he has since written over 100 novels and several screen plays. War has provided the background for several of his novels, including *Private Peaceful* (2003) and more recently *Shadow* (2010). Now in his sixties, he lives on a farm in Devon, where he runs the charity *Farms for City Children* which he founded in 1976.

Michael Morpurgo has won many awards including The Smarties Book Prize, the Whitbread Award, and the Children's Book of the Year Award, and has had his books adapted for stage, television and film. He was awarded the MBE in 1999 and the OBE in 2006. From 2003 to 2005 he was Children's Laureate.

Facts and figures
First published: 1982.
Runner-up for the Whitbread Award for Children's Books in 1982.
Adapted into a play by Nick Stafford, first staged at London's National Theatre in 2007.
Adapted into a film by DreamWorks Studios 2011 (to be released in 2012).

Guided reading

First reading

The first reading should be used to familiarise the children with the main themes, plot line and characters.

Look together at the cover of the book. Ask the children what they think the story is about – what do they learn from the title, image and back cover blurb? Read together the author's note. Focus on the date of the painting, and explain that 1914 was the year that the First World War, also known as the Great War and the 'war to end all wars', broke out.

Tell the children that the war lasted for four years (1914–18) and was fought between Britain and her allies (France and Russia) and Germany and her allies (Austria-Hungary and Turkey). Establish what the children know about the war, and if any of them has relatives who fought in the war, or have seen films of the trenches. Ensure that they differentiate between the First World War and the Second World War (1939–45).

Chapter 1

Read the first chapter and ask the children to identify the narrative voice (it is written in the first person as the horse recalls memories). Ask: *What is the horse's first memory?* (Being separated from its mother when it was sold at auction.) Can the children suggest what might be the *truest of friendships* referred to in the book blurb? (The friendship between Joey the horse and Albert, his master.)

Chapters 2 to 4

Continue reading through Chapter 2. Pause to ask the children why Albert begins to treat Joey more harshly. (He knows he must learn to pull a plough or his father will not keep him.) Establish why war is looming (Germany has invaded Belgium). Ask: *What does the reaction of Albert's mother suggest?* (That she knows the war will be terrible.) Read on to the end of Chapter 4 and pause to ask the children what we learn about the farm and why Albert's father drinks. (He has money worries.) How does this affect Joey? (He is sold to the British army because the farmer can't afford to keep two horses.) Why do they think Albert's father is so edgy and tense when he makes the sale? (He knows his son will be angry and upset.) Highlight the terms *infantry* and *cavalry* and ask the children if they can explain what they mean. (Foot soldiers and horse-mounted soldiers.)

Chapters 5 to 8

Continue reading but pause before the paragraph beginning *My only consolation…* (Chapter 5) to remind the children of the painting by Captain Nicholls described in the author's note. Can they explain the Captain's misgivings about the war? (Soldiers and their horses will be facing new and deadly weapons such as machine guns and artillery fire.) Read to the end of Chapter 8 and then ask the children to summarise what has happened: Joey has been trained for the cavalry and taken on a ship to France where British forces are fighting against the Germans. In the first cavalry charge, his rider Captain Nicholls is killed, and later when Trooper Warren rides him through the wire, they are captured by the Germans. Ask: *Which character now offers comfort and companionship to Joey?* (The horse Topthorn.)

Chapters 9 to 11

Read on, asking the children to explain how the horses are now being used by the German army. (To pull ambulance carts.) Pause to examine and ask what they think is implied by the sentence *I had seen the same grey faces…* in Chapter 9. (To a horse, there is no difference between the men who fight each other, just their uniforms.) Ask: *How is Joey's life now reminiscent of his past life?* (He is living on a farm, and well cared for by Emilie as he was by Albert.) *What happens to break the idyll of farm life?* (The horses are commandeered by the German army to pull heavy guns.)

Guided reading

Chapters 12 to 15

Read on through the next four chapters, pausing to ask the children to summarise the conditions the horses now face (exhausting hard work, poor rations, icy cold weather, mud and so on). Ask: *What tragedy befalls Joey?* (He loses his best friend Topthorn.) Encourage the children to explain where Joey ends up and why. (He finds himself in no man's land, after fleeing from British shells and tanks.) Ensure that the children understand the term 'no man's land', the land between the trenches occupied by opposing armies.

Chapters 16 to 18

Read to the end of Chapter 16. Can the children explain how Joey ends up on the British side? (The two soldiers toss a coin.) How does their solution contrast with what their governments and armies are doing? (They talk to each other and agree a fair compromise, rather than just fighting and killing each other.) Pause at the start of Chapter 17 to ask how Joey recognises Albert. (By his voice and his whistle.) Which phrases does he use that are familiar? (*'How the divil…'* and *'you old silly?'*) Ask them to explain how Albert and Joey have been reunited. (Albert is now 17 and has joined the Veterinary Corps of the British Army to try and find Joey, as he promised.) Read Chapter 18 and ask: *How does fortune again swing to spoil their joy and threaten their future?* (Joey has contracted the disease tetanus which could kill him.)

Chapters 19 to 21

Read on through Chapter 19, asking the children what Joey's role is now he has recovered. (Hauling veterinary wagons to bring wounded horses back from the Front.) How does Albert's loss of his best friend, David, echo Joey's experience? (He lost his best friend Topthorn.) Ensure that the children understand what the British army's plans are for the horses now that the war is over. (They will auction them off, some to be sold for horsemeat.) Finish the story and discuss how it all comes right, to allow a happy ending. (Emilie's grandfather buys Joey but hands him over to Albert for an English penny because he realises that will be best for Joey.) Then tell the children that over 8 million horses were killed in the war, and many more injured or sold off after the war for horsemeat or to labour as pack animals abroad. Pause to ask the children how the story has made them feel about the war horses.

Second reading

Subsequent readings should be used to explore in more detail how the plot, character and setting are developed. Before you begin reading, ask the children to consider the genre and form of the novel. What kind of novel do they think *War Horse* is? (Adventure, history, realistic, autobiographical?) Encourage them to give reasons for their answers. In what ways is it an adventure? (Hero character goes on a long and difficult journey, facing trials, challenges and twists of fate.) In what ways is it an autobiography or memoir? (Joey is looking back on his own life, and recounting it in the first person.) Elicit that although it is a fictional novel, it is based on historical fact – farm horses *were* bought by the British army as mounts for the cavalry and also to carry munitions and supplies, or to pull artillery or ambulance wagons. Refer to any other novels by the author that the children may already be familiar with, that are also based on historical fact and have war-time settings or connections (such as *Private Peaceful*, *Kensuke's Kingdom* and *The Amazing Story of Adolphus Tips*).

Plot structure

Encourage the children to consider as they read what gives structure to the plot. Challenge them to identify plot triggers, such as Albert's father needing money or the war bringing change to the rural community. Joey's memoirs can be read as a journey, both physical from England to France and back, and emotional, from young farm horse to experienced and weary war horse. They can explore what gives structure to that journey, such as changing locations, new owners, and different jobs that Joey is employed to do. Encourage them to identify the twists and turns of fate, and swings of fortune, for example, finding contentment with Emilie on the farm, only to be snatched away to haul artillery to the battlefield, or being reunited with Albert at last, only to succumb to tetanus. The children can also consider the happy ending which brings the plot full circle, as Joey begins and ends his story with Albert on the farm.

Characters

The children should also consider the balance of characters in the novel, both human and equine, and how some provide comfort and friendship to Joey, while others are unkind or hard masters. They should explore Joey's own character, and how it is developed through the first person narrative, which allows us to know not just what happens but what he is thinking and feeling as his adventure unfolds.

Setting

Focus on how Joey is affected by the setting or reacts to it, as he leaves behind the placid fields of rural Devon to travel through the bleak, shattered landscape of the Front. Encourage the children to reflect on how the author filters descriptions of the landscape through Joey's eyes – for example, he sees the approaching army tanks as great grey monsters.

Shared reading

Extract 1

- Read the extract and invite the children to explain what Joey is describing (the British cavalry charging towards the wire marking German lines in battle).
- Ask: *What is implied by* an invisible foe*?* (The German soldiers are hidden in trenches.)
- Explore any unfamiliar vocabulary (such as *foe, galvanised, inexorably, carnage*) asking the children if they can suggest definitions or replacements. Differentiate technical or military terms – *sabres, bombardment* and *squadron*. Explain that the word *bedlam,* suggesting chaos and disorder, originates from Bethlem, a psychiatric hospital for people with mental illnesses.
- Examine how the author creates pace, asking them to highlight strong active verbs that suggest movement (*reared, erupted, stumbled, charged, galloped*) and noise (*screamed, whined, roared*).
- Challenge the class to find alliteration which adds pace (*galvanised myself into a gallop, the bedlam of battle, curses as he saw the carnage*).
- What simile suggests how it felt braving the explosions (*...every explosion seemed like an earthquake*)?

Extract 2

- Read Extract 2 and explore unfamiliar vocabulary (*crump, lumbering, belched, inexorably, sapped*).
- Ask the children to describe how the tank appears to Joey (*a great grey lumbering monster*).
- Revise the idea of personification (describing an inanimate object in terms of a living creature). Challenge them to pick out words that personify the tanks and explain what they mean (*lumbering, belched*).
- Which of Joey's senses alert him to the approaching tanks? (His hearing.) Can they pick out the words that describe sounds? (*Crump,* *whistle, whining, rattle, grating, roaring.*)
- Ask: *How does Joey react and why?* (He panics and flees, because they are unfamiliar and believes they are chasing him.) *What words suggest his panic?* (Such as, *blind terror, bolted, crashed.*)
- Focus on the last paragraph and underline the present participle verbs (*crossing, galloping, jumping, clattering, grazing*). Challenge the children to try replacing the participle form with simple past verbs ('I crossed', 'I galloped', 'I jumped' and so on) and explore how it changes the passage, making it more staccato and less pacey.

Extract 3

- Read Extract 3 and explore unfamiliar vocabulary, asking the children to suggest meaning (*crescendo, interspersed, vantage point, impenetrable, methodically, consternation*).
- Can they explain where Joey is (in no man's land) and what this was? (The land between the trenches of the opposing armies along the Western Front in France.)
- Challenge them to suggest their own words to describe the landscape ('bleak', 'deserted', 'barren'). How has it become a *blasted wilderness*? (It has been constantly shelled.)
- Ask: *What is the first thing that tells Joey people are near?* (He hears voices and laughter.) *How are* *his other senses alerted?* (He sees their helmets and smells food.)
- Focus on the description of the cooking smells, highlighting words that make it sound inviting (*savour, sweetest*). Why would it be so appealing to Joey? (He is exhausted and hungry.)
- Ask the children if they can identify which army the soldiers emerge from in turn (the German, then the British) and cite their reasons (the Germans wore grey, the British wore khaki uniforms). Remind them that to Joey, they are all just men who might offer food. Suggest that his situation can be seen as symbolic: he is an impartial observer, without partisan feelings.

Extract 1

Chapter 8

We were into a canter now and still there was no sound nor sight of any enemy. The troopers were shouting at an invisible foe, leaning over their horses' necks, their sabres stretched out in front of them. I galvanised myself into a gallop to keep with Topthorn and as I did, so the first terrible shells fell amongst us and the machine guns opened up. The bedlam of battle had begun. All around me men cried and fell to the ground, and horses reared and screamed in an agony of fear and pain. The ground erupted on either side of me, throwing horses and riders clear into the air. The shells whined and roared overhead, and every explosion seemed like an earthquake to us. But the squadron galloped on inexorably through it all towards the wire at the top of the hill, and I went with them.

On my back Trooper Warren held me in an iron grip with his knees. I stumbled once and felt him lose a stirrup, and slowed so that he could find it again. Topthorn was still ahead of me, his head up, his tail whisking from side to side. I found more strength in my legs and charged after him. Trooper Warren prayed aloud as he rode, but his prayers turned soon to curses as he saw the carnage around him. Only a few horses reached the wire and Topthorn and I were amongst them. There were indeed a few holes blasted through the wire by our bombardment so that some of us could find a way through; and we came at last upon the first line of enemy trenches, but they were empty. The firing came now from higher up in amongst the trees; and so the squadron, or what was left of it, regrouped and galloped up into the wood, only to be met by a line of hidden wire in amongst the trees. Some of the horses ran into the wire before they could be stopped, and stuck there, their riders trying feverishly to extract them.

Text © 1982, Michael Morpurgo.

Extract 2

Chapter 15

I remember it was near first light and I was cropping the grass close to where they lay when I heard through the crump and whistle of the shells the whining sound of motors accompanied by a terrifying rattle of steel that set my ears back against my head. It came from over the ridge from the direction in which the soldiers had disappeared, a grating, roaring sound that came ever nearer by the minute; and louder again as the shelling died away completely.

Although at the time I did not know it as such, the first tank I ever saw came over the rise of the hill with the cold light of dawn behind it, a great grey lumbering monster that belched out smoke from behind as it rocked down the hillside towards me. I hesitated only for a few moments before blind terror tore me at last from Topthorn's side and sent me bolting down the hill towards the river. I crashed into the river without even knowing whether I should find my feet or not and was half-way up the wooded hill on the other side before I dared stop and turn to see if it was still chasing me. I should never have looked, for the one monster had become several monsters and they were rolling inexorably towards me, already past the place where Topthorn lay with Friedrich on the shattered hillside. I waited, secure, I thought, in the shelter of the trees and watched the tanks ford the river before turning once more to run.

I ran I knew not where. I ran till I could no longer hear that dreadful rattle and until the guns seemed far away. I remember crossing a river again, galloping through empty farmyards, jumping fences and ditches and abandoned trenches, and clattering through deserted, ruined villages before I found myself grazing that evening in a lush, wet meadow and drinking from a clear, pebbly brook. And then exhaustion finally overtook me, sapped the strength from my legs and forced me to lie down and sleep.

Text © 1982, Michael Morpurgo.

Extract 3

Chapter 16

FROM BOTH SIDE OF ME I HEARD A GRADUAL crescendo of excitement and laughter rippling along the trenches, interspersed with barked orders that everyone was to keep their heads down and no one was to shoot. From my vantage point on the mound I could see only an occasional glimpse of a steel helmet, my only evidence that the voices I was hearing did indeed belong to real people. There was the sweet smell of cooking food wafting towards me and I lifted my nose to savour it. It was sweeter than the sweetest bran-mash I had ever tasted and it had a tinge of salt about it. I was drawn first one way and then the other by this promise of warm food, but each time I neared the trenches on either side I met an impenetrable barrier of loosely coiled barbed wire. The soldiers cheered me on as I came closer, showing their heads fully now over the trenches and beckoning me towards them; and when I had to turn back at the wire and crossed no man's land to the other side, I was welcomed again there by a chorus of whistling and clapping, but again I could find no way through the wire. I must have criss-crossed no man's land for much of that morning, and found at long last in the middle of this blasted wilderness a small patch of coarse, dank grass growing on the lip of an old crater.

I was busying myself at tearing the last of this away when I saw, out of the corner of my eye, a man in a grey uniform clamber up out of the trenches, waving a white flag above his head. I looked up as he began to clip his way methodically through the wire and then pull it aside. All this time there was much argument and noisy consternation from the other side; and soon a small, helmeted figure in a flapping khaki greatcoat climbed up into no man's land. He too held up a white handkerchief in one hand and began also to work his way through the wire towards me.

Text © 1982, Michael Morpurgo.

Plot, character and setting

The Great War

> **Objective:** To distinguish between everyday use of words and their subject-specific use.
> **What you need:** Copies of *War Horse* and photocopiable page 15.
> **Cross-curricular link:** History.

What to do

● Re-read Extract 3 and ask the children to explain the concept of no man's land (the land between the trenches occupied by opposing armies).
● What else have the children learned about the First World War from the novel? Encourage them to talk about the British and German armies, the trenches, weapons and transport, how horses were used and so on. Highlight any terminology associated with war in general, (*bombardment,*

artillery, shelling) or with this war in particular (*trench warfare, no man's land*).
● Ask the children how they think the author may have researched the war (by reading books about it, looking at films, listening to people talking about their memories of the war).
● Hand out photocopiable page 15 and invite them to use their knowledge from the novel to write a definition of each term.

> **Differentiation**
> **For older/more confident learners:** Invite the children to research more terms or facts about the war from the novel and add them to their sheets.
> **For younger/less confident learners:** Limit the children to explaining only two of the terms and allow them access to dictionaries and/or websites.

War Haiku

> **Objective:** To select words and language drawing on their knowledge of literary features and formal and informal writing.
> **What you need:** Copies of *War Horse*, images of the First World War Front (photographs, film or paintings), whiteboard, individual whiteboards and pens.
> **Cross-curricular links:** Art, geography.

What to do

● Re-read Extract 3 and ask the children to describe the landscape of no man's land using their own words. What do they think the French countryside might have been like before the war, and what has been destroyed by war? (Grass, flowers, insects, crops, trees and so on.)
● Show the children pictures of the Front, and invite responses. Ask: *What words or phrases would you use to describe the way the landscape looks?* (Shattered, war-torn, bleak, empty, bare.)
● Arrange the children into small groups and highlight passages in the novel that describe the terrain and weather (see Chapters 8, 12, 15 and 16). Ask each group to scan one

chapter, noting down on their whiteboards key nouns (*craters, shells, mud*), adjectives (*wasted, shattered*) and phrases (*laid waste, blasted wilderness*) that describe the landscape.
● Capture key words and phrases on the whiteboard and then challenge the children to compose haiku-style poems to describe the war landscape. Model an example before they begin to ensure they understand the 5-7-5 syllable haiku form. For instance:

> 'Wasted wilderness
> No birds, no trees, no insects
> Just mud and more mud.'

● Invite volunteers to share their poems.

> **Differentiation**
> **For older/more confident learners:** Encourage the children to use techniques such as alliteration, assonance and onomatopoeia in their poems.
> **For younger/less confident learners:** Review the words and phrases the children have collected, discussing possible effects. Also, provide the first line to start their poem.

Plot, character and setting

History and happenings

> **Objective:** To understand how writers use different structures to create coherence and impact.
> **What you need:** Copies of *War Horse* and photocopiable page 16.
> **Cross-curricular link:** History.

What to do
● Begin by telling the children that the author once said that he found inspiration for his stories in things around him: 'big happenings, little happenings and history'.
● Can they suggest examples of each of the above in the novel? (Big happenings such as the British army commandeering horses for the war, little happenings such as Albert's father buying a horse at auction and history such as the outbreak of the First World War.)

● Arrange the children into pairs and hand out photocopiable page 16. Tell them that they need to explain the action that follows as a consequence of each plot trigger or event. They should then cut and paste the action/events in the order they appear in the plot.
● When they have finished, discuss which events on the sheet might be described as big happenings, little happenings and history.

> **Differentiation**
> **For older/more confident learners:** Challenge the children to add more big and little happenings to the sequence of events.
> **For younger/less confident learners:** Help the children to locate the plot triggers in the novel by providing chapter and/or page references.

Timelines

> **Objective:** To understand how writers use different structures to create coherence and impact.
> **What you need:** Copies of *War Horse*, examples of timelines, individual whiteboards and pens.
> **Cross-curricular link:** History.

What to do
● Discuss the narrative form of the novel, and how Joey recalls events in chronological order. Ask the children what genres of writing usually take this form (recounts, historical fiction, biographies and autobiographies).
● Ask the children how much time they think the novel covers, citing evidence from the text. (Joey is sold to Albert's father a few years before the war, which starts in 1914 and lasts for four years.) Elicit that we are talking about a period beginning around 1911 or 1912.
● Ask the children to suggest what helps to give the narrative structure (Joey's different owners,

the places he lives, the jobs he does).
● Arrange the children into small groups and tell them to design a timeline showing the period the novel covers, and marking in significant events in Joey's story. If possible, refer to examples of timelines.
● Review when and how timelines are useful, in mapping out key dates and timescales and discuss different design features that can be used, for example, colours, images, interactive features.

> **Differentiation**
> **For older/more confident learners:** Encourage the children to use ICT to develop their timelines, adding significant First World War dates from their own research, such as important battles at the Somme or Passchendaele.
> **For younger/less confident learners:** Provide the children with a list of key events from the novel to plot on their timelines.

Plot, character and setting

Changing places

> **Objective:** To make notes on and use evidence from across a text to explain events or ideas.
> **What you need:** Copies of *War Horse* and whiteboard.
> **Cross-curricular link:** Geography.

What to do
● Explain to the children that they are going to think about the different places and landscapes that Joey experiences.
● Begin by challenging them to list some of the key locations or places that feature in the novel, capturing them on the whiteboard. For example, Albert's farm in England, the Front, Emilie's farm and the veterinary hospital in France.
● Arrange the children into small groups and assign each group one location. Tell them to scan the novel for key facts about that location, such as where Joey lived, his immediate surroundings and living conditions and what the landscape/terrain was like. They should include any particular memories he has about it.
● When they have finished, let the groups share their information with the class, capturing key information about locations on the whiteboard.
● Debate which places were the most comfortable and happy, and which the toughest or most challenging for Joey to live in, encouraging the children to cite reasons for their answers.

> **Differentiation**
> **For older/more confident learners:** Encourage the children to describe at least two locations using their own words and phrases.
> **For younger/less confident learners:** Provide the children with chapters and/or page references to help them find key information about their location.

Horse for sale!

> **Objective:** To sustain engagement with longer texts, using different techniques to make the text come alive.
> **What you need:** Copies of *War Horse*, whiteboard and photocopiable page 17.
> **Cross-curricular link:** Science.

What to do
● Challenge the children to list in order all the owners/riders that Joey has during the course of his story (Albert's father and Albert, Captain Nicholls, Trooper Warren, Emilie and her grandfather, Friedrich and finally Albert).
● Can they recall how and why Joey changed hands in each case? (For example, by being sold at auction, by his rider being killed or by being commandeered for work.)
● Focus on the two occasions when Joey was sold at auction, first as a young colt to Albert's father and later, to Emilie's grandfather at the end of the story.
● Arrange the children into pairs and hand out photocopiable page 17. Explain that they are going to create an entry for an auctioneer's catalogue, describing Joey. They need to scan the novel for details of his breed, colour and physical markings, as well as his nature and work experience.
● When they have finished, invite volunteer pairs to read out their entries in the style of an auctioneer.

> **Differentiation**
> **For older/more confident learners:** Encourage the children to examine advertisements for horses in local newspapers or on the internet, to add realistic details to their entry such as, wormed and vaccinated.
> **For younger/less confident learners:** Allow the children to focus on Joey's appearance and the jobs he performed.

Plot, character and setting

An emotional journey

> **Objective:** To read between the lines and find evidence for their interpretation.
> **What you need:** Copies of *War Horse*, whiteboard and photocopiable page 18.
> **Cross-curricular link:** PSHE.

What to do

● Tell the children they are going to focus on Joey's character. How do they think he changes from the horse he is at the start of the story, to how he is at the end? (He is just a young colt at the beginning, quite wild and inexperienced, he goes through training, first as a farm horse, then as a war horse, and matures as he goes through the terrible experiences of battle, loss and injury.)

● Can they recall times in the novel when Joey is happy or contented, and times when he is scared or unhappy?

● Hand out photocopiable page 18 and invite the children to fill it in, referring to the novel.

● When they have finished, share some of their ideas from the sheets, and discuss how Joey goes on an emotional journey as well as a physical journey from England to France. Suggest that in some ways for Joey, as for Albert, this is a 'coming of age' story: Albert begins as a young 13-year-old boy on the farm, and grows up to be a young man in the army, just as Joey grows from a feisty young colt into a mature, experienced war horse.

> **Differentiation**
> **For older/more confident learners:** Challenge the children to identify other feelings that Joey experiences, and add them to the sheets, citing situations when he felt that way.
> **For younger/less confident learners:** Provide the children with a list of events for completing 'Situation 2' and discuss the twists and turns in the plot together.

Horse and rider

> **Objective:** To make notes on and use evidence from across a text to explain events or ideas.
> **What you need:** Copies of *War Horse*, whiteboard, individual whiteboards and pens.
> **Cross-curricular link:** PSHE.

What to do

● Challenge the children to list the different riders and grooms who looked after Joey during the course of the story (Albert, Corporal Samuel Perkins, Captain Nicholls, Trooper Warren, Emilie and Friedrich). Who do they think were Joey's favourite riders or grooms? Who were his least favourite? Encourage them to explain their choices.

● Write headings on the whiteboard for good groom/good rider and poor groom/poor rider.

● Ask the children if they can suggest what Joey might appreciate in a good groom/rider such as: will brush and buff his coat, feed him well, ride light on his back. However, a poor groom will overwork or underfeed him, use spurs and keep too tight a rein on him.

● Arrange the children into pairs and tell them to scan the novel and find all Joey's ideas of a good groom and rider, and a poor groom and rider, from his descriptions of how he is treated by different owners. They should note their findings on their individual whiteboards.

● When they have finished, share their ideas under the two headings on the class whiteboard.

> **Differentiation**
> **For older/more confident learners:** Challenge the children to use their notes to draft definitions of a good groom/rider and poor groom/rider, from Joey's point of view.
> **For younger/less confident learners:** Invite the children to concentrate on either a good or bad groom.

The Great War

● Write a definition to explain each of these
First World War terms.

Trench warfare: _____

_____

Shelling: _____

_____

The Front: _____

_____

No man's land: _____

_____

● List three types of weapon from the Great War and briefly explain how
they were used.

1. _____

2. _____

3. _____

● List three types of transport from the Great War and briefly explain
how they were used.

1. _____

2. _____

3. _____

Illustrations © 2011, Stephen Lillie.

Plot, character and setting

History and happenings

● Explain what follows each event and arrange them in the correct order.

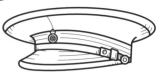

Plot trigger	What does it lead to?
Joey has an infected wound.	
Albert's father attends an auction drunk.	
Emilie's grandfather makes her a promise.	
Albert makes Joey a solemn promise.	
Captain Nicholls is killed.	

SCHOLASTIC
www.scholastic.co.uk

Illustration © 2011, Stephen Lillie.

Horse for sale!

● Fill in this entry describing Joey for an auctioneer's catalogue.

Name
_____

Breed
_____

Colouring
_____

Picture:

Physical markings
_____

Nature/temperament
_____

Training/work experience
_____

_____

_____

Any other details
_____

_____

_____

Plot, character and setting

SECTION
4

An emotional journey

- For each 'Situation 1' listed, decide which emotion Joey is feeling and then think of another situation when he feels the same way.
- When you have filled in the boxes, cut and paste them in the order they appear in the plot.

Emotions				
sad	proud	scared	excited	contented

Emotion	Situation 1	Situation 2
	Joey is parted from his mother.	
	Topthorn dies.	
	Joey is reunited with Albert.	
	Joey and Topthorn lead the cavalry charge.	
	Joey and Topthorn stay on a French farm.	

Talk about it

Earliest memories

Objective: To sustain engagement with longer texts, using different techniques to make the text come alive.
What you need: Copies of *War Horse* and whiteboard.
Cross-curricular links: PSHE, history.

What to do

● Read at pace Chapter 1. Ask: *Do you think the story has a good beginning, and if so why? Why does Joey start by describing the auction?* (It is his earliest memory.) *Why does it stick in his memory?* (It was quite traumatic and emotional for him as he was parted from his mother and sold to a stranger.) Invite a few children to volunteer their own earliest memories.
● Arrange the children into small groups and tell them to discuss their first memories, comparing and contrasting the kind of events they remember. Are there any similarities (for example, significant times like their first day at school, or times when they felt very happy or very sad). Elicit that events that evoke strong emotions often stay with us, as in Joey's case.
● Challenge the groups to invent an earliest memory for another character from the novel, such as Albert, Emilie or Topthorn.
● Invite volunteers from each group to present their idea orally and encourage constructive feedback.

Differentiation
For older/more confident learners: Allow the children to rehearse and present their invented idea as the beginning of an autobiography, in the style of the novel.
For younger/less confident learners: Encourage the children to select the character Albert and to explore the memory of his first day at school or working on the farm.

Talking horses

Objective: To improvise using a range of drama strategies and conventions to explore themes such as hopes, fears and desires.
What you need: Copies of *War Horse*, individual whiteboards and pens.
Cross-curricular link: Drama.

What to do

● Begin by focussing on the narrative voice of the novel, reminding the children that it is written in Joey's words, allowing us to hear his thoughts and feelings. Point out that although Joey speaks directly to us, he cannot communicate with people except in 'nickering' and horse language, nor does he 'talk' to the other horses.
● Explain to the children that they are going to provide the horses' voices by improvising some dialogue between the 'gun team' in small groups. Ask them to prepare by reading Chapters 12–13. They should write a 'cast list' on their whiteboards, noting any key facts about characters, and also key information about the team's work/living conditions.
● Allow the groups time to plan and rehearse a scene in which the horses voice their thoughts and feelings. They should imagine that the horses are communicating with each other as they work. Encourage them to think about individual characters, and also what they may be experiencing and complaining about – hunger, pain, mud, exhaustion.
● When groups are ready, invite them to perform their scene for the class and encourage feedback.

Differentiation
For older/more confident learners: Encourage the children to dramatise their scene using music and sound effects.
For younger/less confident learners: Help the children prepare by highlighting key facts about the gun team horses and their work. Allow them to focus on one chapter/scene.

Talk about it

A case of tetanus

Objective: To make notes on and use evidence from across a text to explain events or ideas.
What you need: Copies of *War Horse* and photocopiable page 22.
Cross-curricular link: Science.

What to do

● Read together Chapter 18. Ask the children to explain what is wrong with Joey and what has caused it. (He has contracted the disease tetanus due to a shrapnel wound.)
● As a shared activity, scan the text extracting Major Martin's instructions for Joey's treatment. Compile a list of instructions, suggesting suitable imperative verbs, such as:
  ● Rig up a sling to support limbs.
  ● Construct a bed of short clean straw.
  ● Black out all windows.
  ● Feed on milk and oatmeal gruel.
● Review the instructions together, checking that they are complete, and that the children are happy with the order and how they are set out.
● Provide photocopiable page 22 and tell the children to create a medical factsheet about tetanus, using the information in Chapter 18.

Differentiation
For older/more confident learners: Encourage the children to do further research about tetanus on the internet or using books, and add any key information to their sheets.
For younger/less confident learners: Allow the children to focus on completing just the main symptoms of tetanus.

Working horses

Objective: To identify and report the main points emerging from discussion.
What you need: Copies of *War Horse* and photocopiable page 23.
Cross-curricular link: History.

What to do

● Ask the children to recall, without referring to the novel, all the different jobs that Joey does during the course of the story – in war and peacetime. (Pulling a plough, cavalry horse, pulling ambulance wagons and heavy guns, hauling carts around the veterinary hospital, then veterinary wagons.) Which do they think he enjoyed most and which least? Encourage them to give reasons.
● Discuss how horses once did many jobs that machines now do, and what has replaced them – tractors and combine harvesters on farms, motorised transport like ambulances, buses, cars and so on. Remind the children that even today machine power is quantified as 'horsepower' (the equivalent number of horses).
● Arrange the children into pairs and hand out photocopiable page 23. Tell the children to discuss and complete the sheet, referring to the novel to help them.
● Review their answers as a class, inviting volunteers to present their work.

Differentiation
For older/more confident learners: Ask the children to discuss in more detail the conditions and challenges that war horses faced, and reflect on how well they think they were treated by both armies.
For younger/less confident learners: Encourage the children to discuss in their pairs the best and worst jobs that Joey did, rating them in order and citing their reasons.

Talk about it

Animals in war

Objective: To use the techniques of dialogic talk to explore ideas, topics or issues.
What you need: Copies of *War Horse*, whiteboard, individual whiteboards and pens.
Cross-curricular link: History.

What to do

● Tell the children that as well as horses, other animals including dogs, pigeons and elephants were used in the First World War. Can they guess what other animal's jobs might have been? (Dogs and pigeons were used to carry messages; elephants hauled heavy equipment.) Explain that many animals were killed by shells or machine gun fire – an estimated eight million horses died.

● Ask the children what they think about using animals this way. Explore the rights and wrongs, encouraging them to give their reasons; for example, can it be right to use animals in war when they have no say and can't decide for themselves? Might there be evidence that animals sometimes enjoy the challenge and camaraderie of work?

● Arrange the children into small groups and ask them to discuss and compile a list of basic rights for animals used in war (such as adequate shelter, food, water, veterinary care, rest and a proper retirement). Ensure they capture their ideas on their whiteboards.

● When they have finished, ask groups to share their ideas and compile a definitive class list of war animals' rights.

Differentiation
For older/more confident learners: Invite the children to discuss what they think the author's views are on war horses and to write a paragraph about it, citing evidence from the novel.
For younger/less confident learners: Ask the children to decide and focus on what they feel are the most essential needs for a war horse and explain why.

Views of war

Objective: To infer writers' perspectives from what is written and from what is implied.
What you need: Copies of *War Horse* and photocopiable page 24.
Cross-curricular links: History, citizenship.

What to do

● Ask the class: *What do you think the author's views are about the First World War? How do you think the loss of lives, human and animal, makes him feel?* (Sad, angry, puzzled, upset?) Challenge the children to cite evidence from the novel to support their answers.

● Can they identify sad events in the novel? (For example, horses and men being killed and injured, in particular, the deaths of Captain Nicholls, Topthorn, Friedrich and David.)

● Ask the children to suggest which characters might reflect the author's own views of war. (Captain Nicholls, Friedrich?) Again, invite them to support their answers with textual evidence.

● Encourage the children to express their own thoughts and views of the war, based on the novel and any other sources.

● Arrange the children into groups of six, supply photocopiable page 24 and ask them to analyse the six characters deciding on their thoughts about the war.

Differentiation
For older/more confident learners: Ask the children to add two speech bubbles and write what the author and Albert might say about the war.
For younger/less confident learners: Allow the children to focus on just three of the characters listed on the photocopiable sheet.

Talk about it

A case of tetanus

● Use the novel to help you fill in this information sheet about the disease tetanus.

Disease: Tetanus

Common name:

_____

Main symptoms:

_____

_____

Causes of disease:

_____

_____

Instructions for treating a horse with tetanus

1. _____

_____

2. _____

_____

3. _____

_____

4. _____

_____

Illustration © 2011, Stephen Lillie.

Talk about it

Working horses

● In pairs find information in the novel to help you complete this sheet.

What did the army vets look for in a prospective warhorse?

_____

_____

Describe the training that horses were given.

_____

_____

List four jobs that horses did in the war and briefly explain them.

1. _____

_____

2. _____

_____

3. _____

_____

4. _____

_____

List three of the key dangers and difficulties horses faced that could injure or kill them.

1. _____

2. _____

3. _____

Talk about it

Views of war

● Write down what you think these six characters might say about the war.

Captain Nicholls

Albert's mother

Friedrich

The Welsh soldier

Emilie

Maisie

Get writing

Cavalry charge!

Objective: To experiment with the visual and sound effects of language, including the use of imagery, alliteration, rhythm and rhyme.
What you need: Copies of *War Horse*, photocopiable page 28, Tennyson's poem 'The Charge of the Light Brigade', copies of Extract 1 (page 8), images and/or film showing a cavalry charge.
Cross-curricular links: History, drama.

What to do
● Read together the description of the cavalry charge from *The order was given to draw swords…* to *…both captains breathless with exertion* (Chapter 5), then re-read Extract 1. Ask the children what is different about each occasion. (The first is training practice; the second is the heat of battle.)
● Tell the children they are going to try writing a poem that captures the drama of a cavalry charge. If possible, read to them Tennyson's poem 'The Charge of the Light Brigade', explaining that it describes a cavalry charge in 1854. Highlight some literary features such as rhythm, rhyme, repetition and alliteration. Display images or film of cavalry charges, encouraging them to describe what they see.
● Arrange the children into pairs and hand out photocopiable page 28 to help plan their poem.
● Allow them time to fill in the sheets, then challenge the children to work independently to draft and edit a poem describing a cavalry charge in the Great War.

Differentiation
For older/more confident learners: Encourage the children to use devices such as repetition and alliteration in their poems.
For younger/less confident learners: Model a few lines of a poem to get the children started, such as: *The flash of the swords/The slash of the sabres.*

A letter home

Objective: To vary the pace and develop the viewpoint through the use of direct and reported speech, portrayal of action, selection of detail.
What you need: Copies of *War Horse* and whiteboard.
Cross-curricular link: ICT.

What to do
● Read Chapter 17 together. Tell the children they are going to write a letter that Albert might write home to his father, telling him that he has been reunited with Joey at last. Briefly revise how to set out and frame a letter.
● Remind them that the episode is narrated by Joey, but now they need to recount the action from Albert's point of view.
● Discuss how Albert would be feeling as he writes the letter (happy, surprised, excited). Encourage them to think what else the letter might contain. (For example, Albert might ask about his mother, Maisie, the farm, or tell his father how his work/the war is going.)
● Invite the children to scan Chapter 17, writing down salient facts (the state the horse arrives in, the Sergeant's instructions, what David says as they clean the horse and the moment at which Albert realises it *is* Joey). Encourage them to note Albert's reactions, as at first he does not believe it, and then as realisation gradually dawns.
● Allow the children time to draft and edit their letters, then encourage volunteers to read them out. Invite constructive criticism and feedback from the class.

Differentiation
For older/more confident learners: Allow the children to draft and develop letters in an old font using ICT skills.
For younger/less confident learners: Scan Chapter 17 as a shared activity, noting salient facts on the whiteboard and help the children begin drafting their letters.

Get writing

Great War horses

Objective: To introduce, develop and conclude paragraphs appropriately, in non-chronological writing.
What you need: Copies of *War Horse*.
Cross-curricular link: History.

What to do
● Ask the children how much they have learned about how horses were used during the First World War by reading the novel. Highlight a few key facts and capture them on the whiteboard, for example:
  ● 'Used by both the British and German armies.'
  ● 'Used to pull guns, veterinary and ambulance wagons.'
  ● 'Many were injured or killed by shells, machine guns, wire or exhaustion.'
● Explain that they are going to write a non-chronological report about horses in the Great War, using information from the novel. Before they begin, revise some of the key features of report writing: formal language, present tense, third person, generic participants and so on.
● Point out that as they will be writing in the present tense, the report will seem contemporary to the war, for example: 'Both armies are using horses to pull guns.'
● Allow the children time to scan the novel for information and draft and edit their reports.
● Invite volunteers to read their reports to the class and encourage feedback.

Differentiation
For older/more confident learners: Encourage the children to research animals used in war using books or the internet and add information to their reports.
For younger/less confident learners: Provide specific chapter or page references to help the children locate key information.

Helping heroes

Objective: To use different narrative techniques to engage and entertain the reader.
What you need: Copies of *War Horse* and images of the First World War Blue Cross fundraising posters.
Cross-curricular link: History.

What to do
● Tell the children that in 1912, shortly before the outbreak of war, a Blue Cross Fund was launched to assist animals in times of war. If possible display images of posters used to raise funds for war horses and encourage the children to identify persuasive techniques (emotive images and language – 'They've done their bit… won't you do yours?').
● Arrange the class into small groups. Explain that they are going to prepare the script for a short film to help the charity raise money for the war horses. They should begin by deciding what their film will show (cavalry horses, a gun or ambulance team) what facts they need to get across (the terrible conditions and dangers horses face, such as mud, exhaustion, shrapnel wounds, tetanus) and what persuasive wording they will use to persuade viewers to pledge money to the fund.
● Allow groups time to prepare and write a script for the voice-over to their film.
● Invite volunteers from each group to outline their film content and read their script. Encourage discussion and feedback from the class.

Differentiation
For older/more confident learners: Invite them to develop a fuller treatment or brief for their film, including images, sound and music.
For younger/less confident learners: Allow the children to try recording their scripts, to develop appropriate tone and manner.

Get writing

Who's who?

> **Objective:** To sustain engagement with longer texts, using different techniques to make the text come alive.
> **What you need:** Copies of *War Horse*, whiteboard and photocopiable page 29.
> **Cross-curricular link:** PSHE.

What to do

● Challenge the children to list the key characters in the novel (both people and horses), arranging them in order of importance to Joey and to the plot line. (Albert and his father, Topthorn, Emilie and her grandfather, Captain Nicholls, Trooper Warren, Friedrich, the gun team and so on.)

● Arrange the children into pairs and hand out photocopiable page 29. Explain that they need to identify each character from the brief notes describing them, then add some more words and phrases that could be used to describe them.

For example, the children could extend the description of Captain Nicholls with the following phrase 'A fine cavalier and an honest man who keeps his word'.

● Let the children complete the sheet with their partner, referring to the novel to help them.

● When they have finished, bring the class together and invite volunteers to read out their character notes. Encourage the children to offer constructive feedback.

> **Differentiation**
> **For older/more confident learners:** Challenge the children to expand their notes for one or two characters and draft short paragraphs describing them.
> **For younger/less confident learners:** Identify one of the characters as a shared activity and model some character notes on the whiteboard such as, *'Friedrich: gentle, talks to himself, anti-war in nature'.*

Heroes' homecoming

> **Objective:** To select words and language drawing on their knowledge of literary features and formal and informal writing.
> **What you need:** Copies of *War Horse*, whiteboard and photocopiable page 30.

What to do

● Read together the last page of the novel, starting *And so I came home…*

● Explain to the children they are going to imagine that they are local newspaper reporters, and that they are going to write a front-page report describing the return of Albert and Joey from the war.

● Discuss what the newspaper report would contain, noting key ideas on the whiteboard for example: the heroes' welcome organised by the villagers, with church bells and silver band; an interview with Albert or his parents, or villagers who know the family.

● Suggest that Albert might tell the reporter about how he first came to know Joey and about the special relationship that they had. He might also tell him about his extraordinary reunion with Joey at the veterinary hospital, and the state that Joey was in. Point out, however, that Albert would not know everything that has happened to Joey, other than the fact that he went to war and what Emilie's grandfather told him.

● Hand out photocopiable page 30 for the children to complete.

> **Differentiation**
> **For older/more confident learners:** Invite the children to develop their newspaper reports using ICT skills.
> **For younger/less confident learners:** Allow the children to discuss the newspaper report and complete the sheet in pairs.

Get writing

SECTION
6

Cavalry charge!

● Plan an exciting poem about a cavalry charge.

Which words describe how the horses move?

_____

_____

What weapons do the soldiers carry? Use words, phrases or similes.

_____

_____

What dangers/obstacles do the men and horses face?

_____

_____

What sounds can be heard?

_____

_____

● Think of words that alliterate (begin with the same sound) and write them below.

Shells	smoke, stirrups, shattering, shrapnel…
Bombardment	
Hooves	
Gallop	

PHOTOCOPIABLE

PAGE
28

SCHOLASTIC
www.scholastic.co.uk

READ & RESPOND: Activities based on War Horse

Get writing

Who's who?

● Identify the character being described and write in their name. Add more character notes to describe them.

Name: _____	Name: _____
A painter and a kind man	A chatty, tiny frail creature
Name: _____	Name: _____
A young boy, barely past 13	A butcher from Schleiden
Name: _____	Name: _____
A hard, gritty little man	The gentlest of men

Get writing

SECTION 6

Heroes' homecoming

● Plan a newspaper story about Joey and Albert returning to their village.

THE TORRIDGE CHRONICLE

DATE: DECEMBER 1918

Headline:

Photograph brief:

Describe the celebrations.

Write quotes from interviewees, including Albert.

■ SCHOLASTIC
www.scholastic.co.uk

Assessment

Assessment advice

War Horse is one of many novels by Michael Morpurgo which weave historical fact into a fictional storyline. The author uses the horse, Joey, as narrator to show us war from an animal's ingenuous viewpoint, allowing him to impart truths about the futility of war, the pain of loss and the strengths of true friendship in a moving yet unsentimental way.

Read & Respond encourages children to carry out a range of activities to exercise their speaking, listening, reading and writing skills. Begin each lesson by explaining the learning objective and where possible relate it to other literacy and cross-curricular work. Given the subject matter in *War Horse* there is considerable scope for linking into the history curriculum. Assessment should be an on-going process, recording progress and highlighting areas that need improvement. It should be based on contributions in shared class work as well as on written individual or group work. After each lesson, encourage children to assess their own work and that of writing partners, deciding which areas need further practice.

Morpurgo's writing is a rich language resource and children can devise their own assessment activities, collecting and exploring features, such as metaphor and alliteration or devising spelling tests based on topics (for example, military terms) or parts of speech (verbs, nouns, adjectives). Photocopiable page 32 can be used to assess the children's comprehension of the main themes and messages contained within the novel.

Themes and messages

> **Objective:** To compare the usefulness of techniques such as visualisation, prediction and empathy in exploring the meaning of texts.
> **What you need:** Copies of *War Horse* and photocopiable page 32.

What to do
● Ask the children what lasting impressions the novel has left them with, about the First World War, the use of horses (or all animals) in the war and Joey's experiences in particular.
● Reflect with the children on what they have learned about the Great War, 1914–18. Encourage them to support their answers with evidence from the text.
● If any of them has seen the stage play or film of the novel, they might want to include discussion of their impressions and memories of those adaptations, and how successfully they convey the story and feel of the novel.

● During the discussion, encourage the children to analyse *how* the novel has moved or affected them. For example, have they visualised the bleak landscape of war through the author's descriptions? Why is it effective to have Joey as the narrator? (Perhaps knowing what he is feeling and thinking helps us to empathise with him.)
● In what ways is the novel an 'adventure' story – what journey and challenges does Joey face? How does the author encourage us to read on by using devices such as cliffhangers (end of Chapter 7) and foreshadowing (end of Chapter 2)?
● Hand out photocopiable page 32 and explain that they are going to review the novel, distilling its main themes and messages.
● Let the children work individually to complete the sheet, using their knowledge of the novel. When they have finished, they can work in groups to discuss their ideas and review the book generally, in the manner of a book club.

Assessment

Themes and messages

● Explain how these three main themes are represented in *War Horse*.

Theme	How is it presented?
Good companions	
Solemn promises	
Loss and waste	

● What messages do you think the author wants to convey about the following?

The Great War

_____

_____

The horses used in the First World War

_____

_____